Left: "**TURQUOISE *KINTSUGI*¹**"
National Monument,
New Mexico, 2022.

THE WAYFARER

Howdy Good Wayfarers,

Sit down around the fire with us, we have some news to share! *The Wayfarer* is expanding into a weekly digital publication. We've launched *The Wayfarer* on Substack!

Since 2012, *The Wayfarer* has been offering literature, interviews, and art with the intention to inspire our readers, enrich their lives, and highlight the power for agency and change-making that each individual holds. By our definition, a wayfarer is one whose inner-compass is ever-oriented to truth, wisdom, healing, and beauty in their own wandering. Our mission as a publication is to foster a community of contemplative voices and provide readers with resources and perspectives that support them in their own journey.

In our effort to continually expand and evolve, we now offer several ways to subscribe!

- Free subscriptions (Access to Monthly public posts.)
- Paid on Subscription
- Print Edition 1yr Subscription

The paid Substack subscription will give unrestricted access to new features, poems, book reviews, recommendations, live readings, and interviews; along with full access to the archive; and access to our new community chats.

Individual Past Print Issues are Available in paperback and ebook on our website as well as Amazon, B&N, Bookshop.org, and more.

Come explore and Subscribe!

Safe Journeys

—Wayfarer Staff

FOUNDER AND EDITOR-IN-CHIEF

L.M. BROWNING

MANAGING EDITOR

HEIDI BARR

EDITORS

THEODORE RICHARDS

IRIS GRAVILLE

ERIC D. LEHMAN

AMY NAWROCKI

DAVID K. LEFF

EDITORS-AT-LARGE

FRANK INZAN OWEN

JASON KIRKEY

KRISTEN WILLIAMS

CONTACT US

WAYFARER@HOMEBOUNDPUBLICATIONS.COM

Published in 2023 by Wayfarer Books

Cover Design and Interior Design by Leslie M. Browning

Photography © Leslie M. Browning / Connor L. Wolfe

trade paperback 978-1-956368-55-0 | ebook 978-1-956368-51-2

PO Box 1601, Northampton, MA 01060

860.574.5847 | info@homeboundpublications.com

HOMEBOUNDPUBLICATIONS.COM & WAYFARERBOOKS.ORG

4

Cavate, Frijoles Canyon,
New Mexico, 2022.

LETTER FROM THE EDITOR

In this special edition of *Wayfarer Magazine*, Frank Inzan Owen suggests we're in a time "that requires everyone to stretch a bit. Stretch to learn. Stretch to educate. Stretch to understand—because massive cultural change is undoubtedly happening." He believes, (as do I), that such stretching requires us to hear people's stories.

Stretching is the opportunity we're given in *Far Rider: Field Notes on Gender Identity, Facing Intergenerational Trauma, and Seeking Awe in the High Desert*, Frank's interview with poet L.M. Browning. These two writers and long-time friends invite us to listen in on their intimate and thoughtful conversation about changing internal landscapes. They explore the ways, as Les describes, that, "Language is a tool that helps us connect to ourselves." You'll discover, though, that these explorations go far beyond adding new words to our vocabulary.

The world of words is familiar territory to Les as readers of *Wayfarer Magazine* know. The founder of Homebound Publications (and its imprints—Wayfarer Books & Magazine, Little Bound Books, Owl House Books, Navigator Graphics) as well as the author of books of poetry, essays, and fiction, Les understands well the power of language. While Les has explored many of life's big questions through writing since the age of 16, the past year has brought new growth regarding identity. As you'll read, this interview marks the last of its kind with L. M. Browning. You'll learn about the new name Les will use, not to erase, but to be "more inclusive to the pieces that were always there and went ignored."

For many of us, our names are central to who we are, how we identify, and the internal landscapes we traverse throughout our lives. It's no wonder then, that many people, myself included, at some time sense the names we were given at birth don't "fit." While transitioning to a self-chosen first name thirty years ago, I studied other cultures and religions and learned that changing names is a common practice around the world. During that year of exploration, I was surprised by the number of people in my own circles who'd informally or legally taken a new name. All of our stories of choosing our names were unique. The opportunity to share and learn our journeys deepened my sense of knowing and being known. I appreciate the generosity with which Les adds another account that stretches readers' understanding.

With gratitude, I welcome you to the story Les shares here in conversation with Frank, as well as the journey Connor L. Wolfe's photographs will take you on through the high desert. Together, they connect us to ourselves and each other.

—Iris Graville

Iris Graville (she/her) is the author of four nonfiction books (including two published by Homebound Publications) and is an editor for *Wayfarer Magazine*.

INTRODUCTION

In this special edition of *The Wayfarer,* Editor-at-Large, Frank Inzan Owen (he/him) sits down in conversation with our Founder, L.M. Browning (they/them), to discuss the topics of gender identity, facing Intergenerational trauma, and seeking awe in the high desert.

In late autumn of 2022, Browning hit the road and disappeared into the backcountry of Northern New Mexico. It was here they began sitting with some larger changes they felt brewing—changes around their pronouns, their gender identity, and their creative pursuits moving forward. *Far Rider* is the product of that time spent in the wild.

Buffalo Grazing, Sandia Mountain in the background:
Sandia Pueblo, Albuquerque, New Mexico.

In American society, we aren't particularly accustomed to people changing their names mid-stream in the journey of their life. There's the phenomenon of a woman changing her name after a divorce. There are the occasional notable instances of famous artists exercising creative license with sudden shifts in personal identity (e.g.: "The Artist formerly known as Prince.") Beyond that, however, it simply isn't a regularly appearing feature.

The matter of nom de plumes (pen names) or stage names (in the case of musicians and actors) is another matter. Somehow there is greater latitude granted in this culture to 'men and women of letters' and people in the spotlight. From Ramón Antonio Gerardo Estévez taking the stage name Martin Sheen, to Howard Allen Frances O'Brien a.k.a. Anne Rice writing under the assumed pseudonyms Anne Rampling and A.N. Roquelaure, in the creative world, anything goes.

But, what about changes in gender-identity, and the subsequent name changes that often accompany this process?

Against the backdrop of the current (and growing) tensions that comprise America's culture wars, in this interview—the last of its kind with L.M. Browning—award-winning author, poet, founder of Homebound Publications and Editor-in-Chief of The Wayfarer Magazine—we take up the topics of naming, pronouns, the transformational process around gender-identity (for both individuals and the culture), and the journey that so many are on in their pursuit of healing, justice, and freedom to authentically align with who they are.

—Frank Inzan Owen

FAR RIDER

Field Notes on Gender Identity, Facing Intergenerational Trauma, and Seeking Awe in the High Desert

Poet L.M. Browning in Conversation with Frank Inzan Owen with photography by Connor L. Wolfe

---

Frank: In the summer of 2022, you quietly changed your pronouns from she/her to they/them. Such quiet changes denote much larger internal shifts. Can you speak to the internal changes that led to the outer change?

Les: When I think about the internal "changes" that brought about this outer change—I think it is fair to say, what "changed" in me was my ability to suppress my own needs and my authentic self came to an end.

It wasn't as though I suddenly woke up and "became" nonbinary—I have always been nonbinary. The change that freed me to fully embrace/embody my nonbinary self was my newfound ability to embrace the part of me I was conditioned to feel shame around.

Frank: Understood. Even so, like a wave that finally surfaces, such newfound inner freedom always seems to be preceded by hard-won journeys and deep dives.

Les: Absolutely. Though, crisis has seemingly always forces me into the deep dives. In 2016, the crisis of miscarrying twins acted as the catalyst that shook me out of heteronormative conditioning and I came to terms with the truth that I am gay/queer.

The same type of crisis/catalyst/coming-to-terms cycle happened again last year; though on a much different scale. This time, I was coming to terms with the fact that I am and always have been nonbinary.

Of course, the goal is to be connected to myself enough in the future that self-realization doesn't require a catalyst to shake loose. [Laughs].

But I agree, it is a hard-won journey. Recognizing that I am nonbinary and understanding how this gender-binary culture has repressed my authentic self as been an overwhelming process. And now, coming out as nonbinary has been overwhelming in its own way.

The most frequent reply I received when telling someone I am gay was something along the lines of, "I'm so happy for you. However, coming out as nonbinary/trans the most frequent reply is, "What does that even mean?" or "Why?"

Frank: We seem to be at a real crux point in this culture, with both wide-sweeping changes and equally force-ful resistance to those changes. Some Americans will always resist change. Others are more open but are still getting accustomed to the idea that other cultures and non-Christian religions are just as much a part of the American experience. So, I can imagine—whether or not a nonbinary person wants it—you frequently find yourself in the position of having to be an "educator" or "cultural ambassador" with answering that "why."

Les: Without a doubt. I have found that, repeatedly answering the "why" has pushed me to not only get granular with my feelings but also boil down the successive realizations that are too numer-ous to catalog and bring them into something succinct.

Frank: If it's a topic that is "difficult to catalog", as you say, then it seems we—as a society—are at that point that requires everyone to stretch a bit. Stretch to learn. Stretch to educate. Stretch to understand the "why" because massive cultural change is undoubtedly happening. No simple answers will do. It requires that we hear a person's story. So, without coming at your particular "why" from the vantage point of entrenched binary culture (that suggests you somehow need to justify yourself), what is the luminous, self-enlightening "why" that is your story around gender identity?

Les: The answer to why I chose to change my pronouns and identify as nonbinary—simply put, I chose to do it in order to be more inclusive of myself. And, honestly, as a child of the 80s, the only option I'd ever had was she/her. I was assigned these gender pronouns at birth.

Left: **"SUNSET CANYON"**
Rio Grande Del Norte National Monument,
New Mexico, 2022.

Right: **"THE LOBO"**
Sangre De Cristo Range;
Taos, New Mexico, 2022.

She/her singularly addresses the anatomy of my body as seen through the narrow definition of gender within our current society—a definition that is the narrowest it has been in recorded history, given that hundreds of societies throughout history have recognized more than two genders–male/boy and female/girl.

In recent years, critics of the movement to widen the gender discussion routinely say that the "fashionable thing" right now is to be transgender or to self-identity beyond the binary, like it is some kind of fad that won't truly be integrated into the common vernacular. On the contrary, the re-emergence of the gender spectrum proves once again that these fundamental truths have/will stand the test of time.

For millennia before the Judeo-Christian ethic took over Western culture, gender existed on a spectrum. We have countless examples of there being a third, nonbinary gender recognized.

We find it in the Navajo, the Mamluk Sultanate, and Hawaii (such as with *Hinaleimoana Wong-Kalu*, the subject of the documentary *Kumu Hina*[2]); there are the *Hijras* in India, the Muxe in Mexico, the *Bakla*[3] in the Philippines—

Frank: Indeed. It is my understanding from my early studies in anthropology that most indigenous societies have not only had some sense of "the ones in the middle" (as it is spoken of in Kumu Hina), but that many nonbinary people were revered as a special type of healer, medicine person, shaman, or culture-carrier. Then, of course, there is modern-day Thailand where a third gender (*phet thi sam, sao praphet song,* etc.) is quite common. All of this to say, I imagine some people in Western industrialized countries think this is some kind of new phenomenon but the fact of the matter is it has been around since there have been people.

Les: Precisely.

Frank: Speaking at language for people who identify as nonbinary, at the beginning of your transition, you used the term "Two-Spirited" but I've heard it isn't a term you decided to carry forward. If not Two-Spirited, then what?

Les: So, yeah, "Two-spirited" is an umbrella term for Native peoples whose gender identity is outside of the binary. The term was brought to the sharing circle by Fisher River Cree Nation Elder Dr. Myra Laramee in 1990 at the 3rd Annual Gathering of Native American Gays and Lesbians.[4]

When the shift started happening and my nonbinary nature was becoming undeniable, I was actually simultaneously doing research into my ancestors. I was on the outs with several blood-relations and looking into the other "blacksheeps" within the lineage. Specifically, I was trying to trace back my family line to a particular Abenaki woman.

Growing up, I was told tales of one of my ancestors along the Canadian border marrying an Abenaki woman. After they were married, the pair of them broke off from the family to go their own way—outcast. When I was told this story as a child, the retelling was always ended with a warning not to tell anyone that we had Abenaki blood because the people were "violent people."

I eventually couldn't find any trace of them—it was just too far back. I was hoping I would be able to trace the lineage back; I think I was subconsciously looking for my ancestries to take me in (so to speak) as I individuated from my family line.

Ultimately, the word "Two-spirited" appealed to me because it felt inclusive of other aspects central to my identity, namely the intersection between gender identity and spiritual identity.

Since I was a child, the idea of a larger interconnectedness between all things has been central to my life.

Ultimately, "Two-Spirited" is a word reserved for those within the First Nations so I lack the central qualifier to use it to define myself; however, I trust the ever-progressing language around inclusivity and gender. As we've touched on, the reality of gender beyond the Judeo-Christian binary is old wisdom—our ancestors have held it safe and we are unearthing it and progressing it.

"DIVIDE"
Rio Grande Gorge;
Taos, New Mexico, 2022.

Right: Along the Rio Grande;
Taos, New Mexico, 2022.

Frank: What is your sense of where all of this is going in modern society? It seems, on the one hand, there are some positive shifts happening in the culture, but, at the same time, there is a resulting backlash (i.e. a clash of worldviews).

Les: While there has been progress made to open ourselves back up as a society to the possibility of gender existing outside of the binary, we also find the unresolved shadow-work rearing its head. I think the clearest example of this in recent years would be the progress seen under the Obama administration and the pendulum swing into Trump and the bald-faced re-surfacing of long-held racism.

The gay community has fought hard for tolerance, inclusion, and equality. The Transgender community has been fighting that same frontline battle but gaining less acceptance.

To choose to embrace/embody your authentic self in a society where you are conditioned to hate and exclude those pieces of yourself that exist outside the norm is an act of nonviolent protest in the pursuit of a more complete representation of self.

Despite all the good progress we've made, there still is a very real threat to Transgender people. For all the welcoming, affirming experiences I've had as a queer person, I have experienced very real homophobia and transphobia (beyond the taunts during childhood). In all honestly, on the drive both to and from New Mexico was strained with many triggered moments in the wake of transphobic/homophobic exchanges.

It is a very isolating experience (to be Queer and Trans in this world as it is now).

[Long Pause.]

When I was in New Mexico, I wasn't that far from one of my dearest friends and authors who lives in Colorado Springs. I was supposed to meet up with him on the day of November 20th. I had toyed with the idea of going into Colorado Springs a day early to visit a queer space there—somewhere I could feel a sense of community after. Ultimately, my friend tested positive for COVID and we canceled the meeting. But, on November 20th, when I woke to hear the news of the shooting at Club Q the night before (one of the intended stops), I felt a ghost pass through me and was flooded with valid anger and grief for the Queer/Trans Community. (It should be noted, November 20th also happens to be Transgender Day of Remembrance.)

[LONG PAUSE].

So, I suppose the point is, yes, there is indeed a refreshing new vocabulary around gender, but it is a very old discussion that has been narrowed over the centuries and is finally opening back up due to decades of gay and trans activism. It's hard-won ground and the fight is far from over.

Eagle Rock Lake, Carson National Forest,
Near the Village of Questa; New Mexico, 2022..

Frank: Indeed. This seems a good moment to address the nuts-and-bolts of this discussion for readers who may not be as familiar with nonbinary gender-identity.

Les: Absolutely, I mean, I am sure we could go term for term as we progress through the interview, but I also think it is helpful to have a few terms defined properly. So, I am going to literally open up the HRC (Human Rights Campaign) glossary and just cherrypick a few relevant terms.

Cisgender | A term used to describe a person whose gender identity aligns with those typically associated with the sex assigned to them at birth.

Gender identity | One's innermost concept of self as male, female, a blend of both or neither—how individuals perceive themselves and what they call themselves. One's gender identity can be the same or different from their sex assigned at birth.

Nonbinary | An adjective describing a person who does not identify exclusively as a man or a woman. Nonbinary people may identify as being both a man and a woman, somewhere in between, or as falling completely outside these categories. While many also identify as transgender, not all nonbinary people do. Nonbinary can also be used as an umbrella term encompassing identities such as agender, bigender, genderqueer or gender-fluid.

Sex assigned at birth | The sex, male, female or intersex, that a doctor or midwife uses to describe a child at birth based on their external anatomy.

Gender binary | A system in which gender is constructed into two strict categories of male or female. Gender identity is expected to align with the sex assigned at birth and gender expressions and roles fit traditional expectations.

Transgender | An umbrella term for people whose gender identity and/or expression is different from cultural expectations based on the sex they were assigned at birth. Being transgender does not imply any specific sexual orientation. Therefore, transgender people may identify as straight, gay, lesbian, bisexual, etc.

Gender expression | External appearance of one's gender identity usually expressed through behavior, clothing, body characteristics, or voice, and which may or may not conform to socially defined behaviors and characteristics typically associated with being either masculine or feminine.

Gender non-conforming | A broad term referring to people who do not behave in a way that conforms to the traditional expectations of their gender, or whose gender expression does not fit neatly into a category. While many also identify as transgender, not all gender non-conforming people do.

Gender dysphoria | Clinically significant distress caused when a person's assigned birth gender is not the same as the one with which they identify.

Rio Grande Del Norte
National Monument,
New Mexico, 2022.

Bighorn Sheep, Carson National Forest
Backcountry at 8,700ft near Red River, New Mexico, 2022.

Frank: Having this glossary as a guide sure would have been helpful nearly 30 years ago when I first became a counselor. There simply wasn't this level of awareness available to me back then. It took me having a transgender client in my clinical internship, and then another trans client later, before I was confronted with my own lack of education and understanding. Making the journey with one of those people as they came to their own conclusions was a real gift. It began to open my eyes to just how rigid the conditioning is in this culture.

Les: Yes, there are a series of conclusions and assumptions that the binary construct makes; namely, that there are only two *genders* (male and female), only two *sexes* (male and female), and that your *cisgender* (being physically born a male or female) informs your gender identity.[5]

Society then informs how that specific gender is to be expressed in mainstream culture: (i.e.: girls wear pink, boys wear blue, which is simply the result of an advertising campaign from the 1940s[6]).

However, if we separate *sex* and *gender* as two different things, and recognize that one doesn't inform the other, then we are free to find our authentic selves without having to be mentally constrained by society's conditioning.

That is really the foundational notion. All of this knowledge and language is something I have been exposed to during my travels and in particularly posting-up in queer enclaves where this is all baseline now.

We aren't talking about simply adding new words to our vocabulary; *language* is a tool that helps us connect to ourselves.

[Pause.]

22

Georgia O'Keeffe Private Home & Studio
Abiquiú, New Mexico, 2022.

I was recently listening to an interview with Brené Brown[7] and the question was posed to her, "How do we know if we're connected authentically to ourselves or not?" And her response was, "...it's a question of embodiment. Are we connected to our bodies?" and went on to speak to the importance of having access to expansive language. "Language does not just communicate emotion. Language shapes and changes what we're feeling—language is an active ingredient of our emotions."

So—following that, not being able to connect to our bodies in an authentic way atop being deprived of this expansive language has been emotionally damaging and this new expanding definition of gender and the language around it—getting granular with it all—*literally* is healing us as it brings us to a more comprehensive understanding of self all facilitated by language that is more inclusive of our whole self.

Frank: I definitely comprehend the embodiment aspect of this. It is key. An added aspect that really struck me in my own education and work with a trans person, and then encountering a trans person within an indigenous context, was the spiritual dimension of this. By "spiritual" I mean the multidimensional nature of a person. Spirit, too, is a spectrum and can present in any number of ways. Once I "got" that, not as an intellectual concept but as a lived reality, it became so clear to me why any attempt—by culture, family, government, or religion—to try to bend a person away from their authentic expression is a form of violence to the soul. It's the oldest battle there is, really—the battle for the freedom of the human spirit; and now it seems that battle has become focused with the trans community.

I think it is important to remember that the Transgender community has been on the frontlines of the Gay Rights Movement since its inception. I look to those towering trans pioneers such as Christine Jorgensen, Sylvia Rivera, Miss Major Graffin-Gracy, and Marsha P. Johnson—who were central figures behind the "success" of the Stonewall Riots–even had to fight for equality in the gay community. When attending the first Pride Parade in 1970, Sylvia Rivera attended but was not allowed to speak. She grabbed the mic anyway and said, "If it wasn't for the Drag Queen, there would be no Gay Liberation Movement. We're the front-liners." She was booed off the stage.[8] And, of course, we are still seeing attacks on Drag in the national news.

Obviously, the gay community has *more than* done its work and are *instrumental* allies in Transgender Rights. But the fear-based response to the Trans community is still very real, speaking overall. There feels like there is a growing majority of people who aren't merely opposed to recognizing gender beyond the binary, but who believe, "...all transgenderism should be *eradicated.*"[9]

Left: Courtyard of O'Keeffe's Private Home.
Abiquiú, New Mexico, 2022.

Bottom: Self-Portrait of the Photographer.
Courtyard of O'Keeffe's Private Home.
Abiquiú, New Mexico, 2022.

Frank: Yes. We're at a disturbing place, culturally, which makes education all the more important. What are your thoughts about the most effective means for that education to occur?

Les: Honestly, without going off further down that rabbithole, I think a great place for anyone to start is the Human Rights Campaign (HRC)'s Website. Such good resources.

Frank: Very good. I know folks involved with the HRC. They do good work. So, as you've said, society seems to be progressing to a more open and accepting footing in some ways, with even the American Psychological Association revising its earlier views, and the American Academy of Pediatrics openly urging support and care of transgender and gender-diverse children and adolescents. But, it hasn't always been the case and I can imagine your experiences along the way haven't always been pleasant and that you haven't always felt the freedom to be yourself.

Les: Absolutely. For this kid, from a homogenized, Italian, Catholic small-town in Connecticut, it wasn't an option to be myself. The masculine part of me was barely tolerated, often "othered," or outright mocked and shamed.

Frank: Was there a moment you can remember becoming conscious of the fact that you are nonbinary?

Les: It is hard to say what exactly spurred the awareness. I think it was a confluence of events that brought it about. The realization was in the works for several years. I find that inwardly when we come to more stable/safe points in our life, the larger internal issues we are trying to reconcile shift into high gear.

Frank: So true.

Les: I've found that, when my authentic self is seen and loved and encouraged, that sets the stage for suppressed parts of myself to surface and integrate.

Just that simple act—being given a reason to love a part of myself that I'd been taught to hate, or to be proud of a part of myself I've been taught to feel shame around—gave me the final permission to acknowledge the parts of myself that had been repressed due to mental conditioning.

Left: O'Keeffe's Bedroom. Private Home. Abiquiú, New Mexico, 2022.

Right Top: Kitchen. Private Home. Abiquiú, New Mexico, 2022.

Right Bottom: O'Keeffe's Private Bath and Dressing Room. Private Home. Abiquiú, New Mexico, 2022.

Frank: I've heard other people speak of how they had a sense along the way that they were nonbinary but they simply didn't have the vocabulary for it; and, since they didn't find themselves in a culture that has a wider understanding of gender, like, say, traditional Hawaiian, there also wasn't that ground for self-understanding within the context they found themselves. Without an accommodating culture, without the ground of understanding, and without support, you must have had experiences that left you feeling like a "stranger in a strange world."

Les: Like so many, I was a recipient of homophobic conditioning due to the time in which I was raised. As an 80s child, the gay community was on my radar from a young age due to my mother's activism during the AIDS crisis during the early 90s. Though, throughout my childhood, I interacted with mainly gay men, there were no "lesbians"—no representation for me to see myself reflected back.

Now, of course, as I got older, I understood there was one cis woman named Pam, who identified as "lesbian" but it was downplayed due to the fact that she was a teacher at a Catholic high school and it was known that, if she were to be "outed" she would lose her job—period. Pam served the same school for decades and died unexpectedly a few years ago. She is remembered at that school as one of the true mentors—that teacher you remember; who saw you. Because of homophobia and the fear around the *global pandemic* of AIDS, the 80s were a terrifying time for those in the gay community. And because people like Pam had to hide their authentic selves, the members of the youth communities such as myself, weren't able to witness her truth and feel doors within our own selves open.

Left: "HOLLOW BONE."
Backcountry, Ghost Ranch;
Abiquiú, New Mexico, 2022.

Right: Self-Portrait of the
Photographer; Abiquiú, New
Mexico, 2022.

"...TO ME THEY ARE AS BEAUTIFUL AS ANYTHING I KNOW...
THE BONES SEEM TO CUT SHARPLY TO THE CENTER OF
SOMETHING THAT IS KEENLY ALIVE ON THE DESERT
EVEN THO' IT IS VAST AND EMPTY AND UNTOUCHABLE..."

— Georgia O'Keeffe

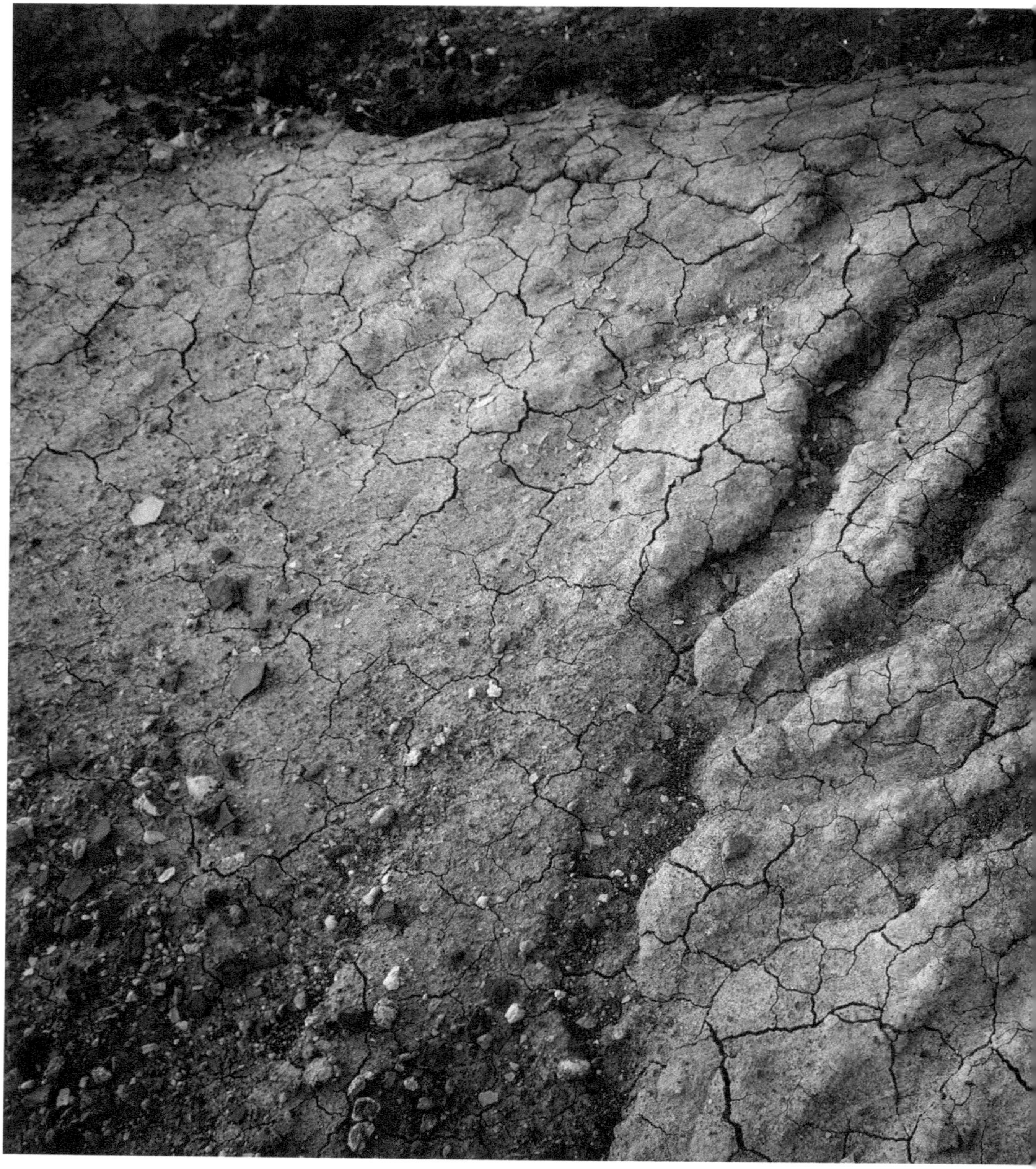

"AFTER BIRTH"

Backcountry, Ghost Ranch,
Abiquiú, New Mexico, 2022.

Frank: This really gets at the heart of the matter about representation. I can remember a very powerful argument made by the author Jerry Mander about *Diné* (Navajo) kids not seeing anyone who looked like them on TV. In that context, not seeing their culture ever represented in the mainstream set up an intrapsychic sense for many of them of being part of a "dead and gone" culture. Never seeing LGBTQIA+ people represented has the same potential effect. Along your own way, did you know nonbinary/trans or lesbian folks? In other words, what was and wasn't represented in your formative years?

Les: There were several personalities represented in my childhood. Most of these were maladaptive presences—people who were caught in their own trauma cycle without the tools and/or capability to help themselves integrate their trauma and move forward and so passed on the pain they couldn't process.

During my childhood, I spent long stretches through the summers with different relations. Each year, I would go here or there while I was out of school. My mother was a single mother working a full-time job, so child care fell to relations willing to host me. I bounced around...so I was exposed to different viewpoints but most of them were not helpful in teaching me how to actually *like* myself.

While spending time with the different generations of my family, there were a number of relations who openly used horrible slurs for different minority groups—the gay community among them. I grew up hearing these words and sensing their meaning, and subconsciously absorbing an inherited hatred of who I am.

I mean, that's how we learn to repress who we are—we sense the judgment, the rejection, the loss, the abandonment that would be suffered if we were to be who we authentically are. And so, the brain does its job—it keeps the organism moving forward and surviving and we repress those parts of ourselves that are undesirable.

"ALONG THE EQUATOR OF PANGAEA"

Backcountry, Ghost Ranch, Abiquiú; New Mexico, 2022.

Frank: So, what have you encountered yourself, now that you have come out as nonbinary?

Les: One of the most frequent responses I've gotten lately to those I've come out to as nonbinary who are my age or older is, "Imagine what it would have been like had we been born now—with the language there is now around sexual identity and gender identity." And it is true, I think about it all the time and it is becoming clearer and clearer to me just how impacted I was by growing up as a deeply queer and nonbinary individual during a time when that wasn't an option offered.

More than once, I can recall gay slurs and hushed whispers when I would spend time with my wider relations. In my high school in the late 90s, when two girls went to prom together, the administration called the police.

"Nonbinary" really wasn't widely used until rather recently. I couldn't be "nonbinary" in the 80s so I was a "tomboy", or worse, I was an *"it."*

I can still remember taking the train into 30th Street [Philadelphia] one day; I was like 12 or 13, I think. A woman sitting in the seat across looked me over with a raised eye, then turned to my mother and bluntly asked, "Is it a boy or a girl?" Still today, I can remember how "othering" her comments felt.

...I felt like...if I couldn't be a "he" and I couldn't pass for a "she" then it meant I would be an "it" —something unloveable, unrelatable...someone who was noticeably odd.

...There were daily reminders like that *conditioning* me to believe that my gender expression was wrong or weird.

Frank: I can imagine in going through the deep process you have, and coming to a point of congruent footing in yourself, that all sorts of other "Hindsight is 20/20" memories may continue to surface around your own levels of self-awareness along the way. What are some of your earliest memories in this regard?

Les: Going all the way back to Kindergarten—every event at school was the same nightmare of trying to find an outfit that would meet the social criteria for feminine dress clothes but didn't make me feel like I was going against the grain of my soul.

I mean, this intertwines throughout my entire life... There is a memory I can still recall being told. It is about when I was a small child—I was 3 or 4. I wandered my way into the bathroom, climbed up to the sink, took my grandfather's razor and shaving my face like I had a beard. I shaved dry—no water and essentially took off the top layer of skin. I did this simply because I was compelled to do so—it just felt right.

I can also recall another story... You know, we all have those handfuls of stories that we are told over and over again—it's like our own personal cosmology. Well, it was *that* memory. Anyway, every year, on my birthday, I would hear the story from some relative or another about how my mother *knew* she was having a baby girl—even before the doctors told her the sex of her child. It's a seemingly loving enough story but in retrospect it pretty much locked my female identity into place and directly tied it to my place in my family. I've had to force myself to re-evaluate such second-hand narratives as I integrate my authentic self, but it is scarer than you think it might be because you're essentially questioning the foundational beliefs you hold about yourself.

[Pause.] ...there are honestly, so many examples.

I never went to prom or homecoming because wearing a dress, make-up, etc. always felt violating–a betrayal of self–and not comforting to those gender norms wasn't an option if I wanted to participate.

I didn't even go to my high school graduation because I wasn't allowed to wear pants. On the day of the graduation rehearsal, the administration told me that I couldn't wear a pair of black dress pants with a button-down shirt to my graduation because it was "inappropriate for a girl to wear pants at a formal event" and I had to "represent myself and my teachers who had gotten me to this day, well."

...That day, I took my diploma, hugged my favorite art teacher (because, I survived school in the art department), and I left—

In retrospect, I felt myself coming up against some larger socially agreed upon set of morals. I knew something was wrong but I didn't have a larger comprehension to understand that I was encountering social and structural violence against people who didn't fit in with the heteronormative world. I was being suppressed into anti-feminist gender roles—wherein–literally–only men could wear the pants. [Laughs]

"PASSING THROUGH"

Backcountry, Ghost Ranch, Abiquiú, New Mexico, 2022.

Frank: I get it, and every instance of attempted entrainment leads to an added layer of the culture (around you at the time) trying to reinforce a structure that goes against your spirit. I'm suddenly thinking of those First Nations people forced into boarding schools, forced to wear the clothes of the oppressor culture, not allowed to speak their own language. A completely different context, but the mechanics of oppression are the same wherever they appear.

Les: Every single time I had to put on a dress, or a skirt, or put my hair up, or wear makeup, or style my hair--I would be in tears. Inwardly, I was going against some core part of myself. Then, on the outside, I was facing consistent bullying at school.

Beyond the people in my neighborhood, I had what we all did: TV, media, literature or the absence thereof. There was few-to-no lesbians in the mainstream other than Ellen, who essentially lost everything by coming out and was publicly rejected.

In the 90s, all I knew about *lesbians* was that it rhymed with *Leslie.* I knew this because I was often bullied with the grating rhymes during middle school--(you know, *just* late enough in my childhood for it to leave a scar but too early to know what it all meant). [Laughs.]

It was decades of such behavior—hundreds of examples—during the most formative years of my life. It takes a toll. In my case, the toll was deep repression—I repressed I was queer, I repressed I was nonbinary, I repressed that I wasn't attracted sexually to men—I repressed that I had needs—I repressed everything.

Flash forward to age 30 and I'm still repressing, (I'm still not conscious that I'm queer let alone nonbinary/transgender) and I had begun reaching to alcohol and drugs to dull the distress of being in my own mind/body. I'd become a compilation of maladaptive coping mechanisms rather than anything resembling my authentic self.

Backcountry, Ghost Ranch,
Abiquiú, New Mexico, 2022.

Frank: So, you have really been on a journey from self-hate to self-love, moving from repression to self-acceptance, self-befriendment, and sovereignty. I really feel the magnitude of this and the fact that your individual journey has implications in terms of the collective. What is your sense of the link between your own shifts and the future-culture?

Les: Completely. When you are raised to hate what you are and society conditions you to hate who you are, you will become an active oppressor of your own becoming. Because you're being given the unspoken-but-very real ultimatum between becoming and belonging.

I believe all the generations prior to this current generation (for whom this is already the norm) —I believe we are being given an opportunity. Now that our journey of social healing and education has progressed to the point that it has, (wherein we have more inclusive language around gender and sexual identity) the opportunity is being given for each individual to return to the foundational gender question and (re)define it for themselves.

The breakdown of heteronormative narratives and the introduction of more expansive language, allow each of us to find those nonbinary/transgender parts of ourselves that were tolerated and othered, bring them forward, integrate them, and reemerge with a more authentic expression of self.

"CRADLE"

Backcountry, Ghost Ranch, Abiquiú, New Mexico, 2022.

Bottom: Backcountry, Abiquiú, New Mexico, 2022.

Backcountry, Ghost Ranch,
Cerro Pedernal Mesa in the distance;
Abiquiú, New Mexico, 2022.

Frank: How was your announcement received by your friends and family? Did it create waves or was your evolution supported?

Les: There were *tsunamis* made. [Laughs].

Yeah. Last year . . . I lost a lot of people–in some form or another. Some died and others simply left.

Those "hard-won" journeys we were talking about earlier—those journeys take us into terrain not everyone is going to choose to traverse with us. Simply saying the words, "I am changing my pronouns" or "I am nonbinary" was a huge, terrifying moment, but even that moment was merely the culmination of a much larger/longer personal journey that was as messy as it was transformative.

I would say, I was supported and I was also abandoned—it isn't all one or the other.

I mean, this past year, I was at my most triggered, the most suicidal, most dissociative, most self-harming–the most unloveable I'd ever been.

Frank: Why do you think that was?

Les: [Pause.] I think *death* and *birth* are the messiest things in this life and last year both were happening to me simultaneously. Breakdown and breakthrough are always so closely linked— death and rebirth come on the heels of each other.

Frank: I comprehend. Like the alchemical inner shiftings and upheavals that can be part of the "falling apart" and "rebuilding" of mid-life, all of this sounds quite initiatory to me.

Les: It certainly is. As I said, I came into this time of realization spurred by crisis. When I came out as nonbinary, it was the summer of 2022. I had just turned 40. It was the quintessential mid-life moment wherein everything came to bear.

The larger gender questions brewing in me aside, it was a year of successive deaths. Within the span of three months, I lost my best childhood friend to suicide, (which, in turn, spurred several repressed memories around childhood abuse and delayed rage to surface). Then I lost another dear, dear friend when a sudden fall claimed the life of poet David K. Leff in late May.

During those months, I lost a lot of long-time friends because they saw my unraveling and equated it to a character flaw rather than mental illness due to a lifetime of trauma.

While the pre-conceived notions around gender are hard to live under, so too are the preconceived notions regarding mental illness. It is astonishing to me the number of people I have met— people who have been educated—who don't believe in mental illness. For me, people who don't believe that mental illness exists are the equivalent of the emotional-flat-earthers—it is an entirely different level of entrenchment.

So, I did lose many friends and family during 2022 but, in retrospect, I think I lost more acquaintances due to the exacerbation of my Complex Post Traumatic Stress Disorder (CPTSD)[10] (and the stigma around mental illness; the lack of trauma-informed services for those in crisis/an exacerbation, etc.) and than to coming out as nonbinary.

Frank: Pardon yet another 'why' question, but, in addition to taking new pronouns, you've decided to take a new pen name. Tell us about this new pen name and what inspired you to adopt it?

Les: Yes. Well, I've found that so much inside of me has shifted, it is time. Strangely, I feel like I've always known I would change my name at some point. It sounds weird to say that, but it is true. I used to think it was just because I was a writer. Like we discussed, in the arts world taking a new name of your choosing isn't as big of a deal.

After high school, when my dyslexia improved and I started reading more, I dove into reading about the various circles of poets and artist—like the Beats, Bloomsbury, the American Transcendentalists, painters like O'Keeffe and Kahlo. And all of these circles were composed primarily of deeply queer individuals who were in non-traditional dynamics/ relationships for their times.

Most creatives are iconoclasts of their time so the creative community lives and breathes the unconventional. It's been a gift really—to move in these circles. When I was younger, I expressed myself in the visual arts. Plainly put, I survived the trauma that was my public education in the art room.

I think being an artist/poet has weirdly helped prepare me for this transition because it has taught me the process of creation. And it has kept me squarely in a world where those who conform are the "odd" ones.

I find, choosing the right company keeps my mind right; whomever I'm talking to on the daily is going to either help keep my mind open or keep it closed. Now, because of my job as a publisher/editor/agent, I am surrounded by iconoclasts, poets, musicians, cowboys, bohemians, storytellers, hippies, vagabonds, artists, shamans—all types and stripes.

5
0

Backcountry, Ghost Ranch,
Abiquiú, New Mexico, 2022.

Frank: What name did you come to for yourself?

Les: I was born, Leslie Marie Browning. Of that name, I am keeping "Les" because I feel like I have made those three letters mean something. "Les" is coming with me in the form of my middle name as a transition into using the name Connor L. Wolfe.

Frank: Les, pronounced as in *less*. Correct?

Les: Correct. And,I tell my friends and colleagues, if you have known me by "Les" and I am inviting you to join me in this next half of my life, you can call me "Les" if it feels right to you or you can call me Connor. Changing my name isn't about erasing who I was it is about being more inclusive to the pieces that were always there and went ignored.[11]

Connor Wolfe is the next vehicle for my creative endeavors. Changing my pen name in addition to my legal name wasn't a decision I made lightly. I've written under L.M. Browning since I first started writing at age 16, which was about three lifetimes ago. It was time. In retrospect, part of me always knew I would change my name. The evolution of Connor Wolfe has been a lifetime in the making.

Some of us carry our future names inside us. Names can be like shirts that we are too small to fit into—and fill-out properly—but that we may one day grow into. This is how Connor came to be, but I also have other names within me that I am growing toward and into that represent other aspects of my path, spiritually, and creatively.

Frank: What has stirred your link to these other names?

Les: Yes, it's strange actually, new names has been a focus for me lately across many fronts. There is this huge shift in me taking the name Connor but I also have had other experiences that add more significance.

In October, I retreated to Northern New Mexico for a few months following the events of the summer. During my time criss-crossing the country, I took part in psilocybin therapy for my severe CPTSD[12].

Each psilocybin session morphed into this internal journey, at the end of which, I was called a name other than "Les." Over the course of three different treatments, I experienced the reciting of this same name—one that I only spoke aloud recently. For a year, I held it tightly against my chest, both treasuring it and fearing it—fearing myself, just fearing everything.

Backcountry, Ghost Ranch, Abiquiú, New Mexico, 2022.

Frank: In some spiritual and poetic traditions (Buddhist, Sufi, indigenous, etc.) a person may be given multiple names over a lifetime, representing different life stages, different creative phases, or different initiatory stages of study. Additionally, in some traditions, a person may receive what's called a "secret name." Unless it is a secret name, do you feel comfortable sharing this other name that made itself known to you in your journey work?

Les: I would view this through the Buddhist lens for sure.

I suppose, for a long time, I think it was a secret name, in that I didn't feel it proper to share it. I felt that way about Connor for a long while. I only started using the name Connor when I returned to Taos. But, like with so many things in my life recently, there has been a shift. The name is, Far Rider.

Far Rider isn't a name I feel I can fully take as my own (yet) because it is still too far away on the horizon. But it speaks to what lies ahead, just the same way Connor did when it manifested through different parts of my earlier life. So, hearing Far Rider in my psilocybin journeys was like glimpsing the *next frontier*–it is out there on the horizon reminding me that I am always growing.

Frank: Far Rider is a good name for a Wayfarer if I've ever heard one! With regard to your overall name change to Connor Wolfe, will there be a difference in writing style or focus with the work you do as compared to the work you did under L.M. Browning?

Les: There are evolutions within my voice as L.M. Browning and there will continue to be new variations. I don't think I fully began finding my authentic voice as a writer until I released my later works. So, I am not taking a new pen name because I am changing genres or because I want anonymity. I am retiring my work under the pen name L.M. Browning, recognizing that enough has happened in my life to constitute a change of name.

Part of me will always be L.M. Browning. Respecting the name and the body of work is the choice to respect a substantial leg of my journey. Allowing that younger self to have their feelings and experiences even though I have continued evolving.

Top: Self-portrait of the Photographer.
Abiquiú, New Mexico, 2022.

Bottom: Backcountry, Ghost Ranch, Abiquiú,
New Mexico, 2022.

"CERRO PEDERNAL"

Backcountry, Ghost Ranch;
Abiquiú, New Mexico, 2022.

Frank: Speaking of horizons, what is the next focus?

Les: I foresee my future work focusing heavily on awe-seeking to alchemizel pain/suffering, and most importantly focusing on unaddressed intergenerational trauma. Yung Pueblo writes that, because of the global availability of healing resources and the psychological education that is part of the mainstream now, we are the "healing generation." I believe this to be true and I believe that we will be a generation who experience a high occurrence of exile and orphanhood due to this role.

Frank: How did you come to focus on intergenerational trauma?

Les: I experienced deep childhood trauma—is where my Complex Post Traumatic Stress Syndrome originated. Following my TEDx Talk on successive trauma at Yale in 2018, I started publicly live with my struggle with CPTSD and suicidal ideation as a way to humanize/normalize the disease.

As I tried to heal from the successive exacerbations of my CPTSD, my personal journey to process and integrate the trauma of my life inevitably led me to the generational trauma in my family line. I should have seen that coming, but I didn't.

[Laughs.] I mean, if you trace your own trauma back to its root, you naturally come to the connecting point wherein you see how your own trauma is (in large part) a result of something done to one of your primary relatives that went unprocessed and projected onto you.

Nutshell Example: Your great-grandparents endure multiple World Wars and a Great Depression–way too much to handle. And then they pass along the unprocessed trauma of those experiences to their children (your grandparents). These children, who now have inherited the psychological effects of their parents' trauma, go on to endure their own personal trauma and large-scale global trauma of Korea and Vietnam. Then they pass their unprocessed trauma onto their children (your parents), who in turn project the unprocessed trauma onto you and so on. This is intergenerational trauma.

It would all be straightforward enough to address openly among the respective generations; however, this is where conditioning comes in–the generations before us were socialized/conditioned to deal with their mental illness through repression–the "we don't talk about it" approach.

Frank: As a Southerner, I fully comprehend the "we don't talk about it" mentality. Besides the "Don't Say Gay" Bill in Florida, we're even seeing this presently with Florida Governor DeSantis' attempts to purge anything in education that discusses diversity awareness, inclusion, or the realities of slavery and Jim Crow in American history. In any context, this entrenchment mechanism of "we don't talk about it" feels like a resistance to inevitable change. It sounds like this was a feature of your family.

Les: Silence, white-washing, repression, gas-lighting, guilt, exploitation, denials—these were all "normalized" features of my family's dynamic. It was very-much a *we-don't-talk-about-it* situation. Then enter someone such as myself... [Laughs].

I have always been that kid at the kitchen table who says the thing that everyone has silently agreed should not be spoken about. The adult manifestation of this character trait is to be the one who brings to the forefront the shadow effects of our unaddressed generational trauma.

As you know with your background in psychotherapy, contrary to popular belief, addressing generational trauma isn't about finding someone to *blame* for a family's psychological inheritance. It is about thoroughly and with compassion, recognizing the traumas of each respective generation—all of which is being subconsciously passed on to the younger generations—so that we can all break free of patterns that no longer service us.

I am the "black sheep" or the "scapegoat child" in some circles among my blood-relations. This vilification by several blood-relations certainly played a role in my decision to take a new name. I didn't make the decision lightly. The resistance I've received from my blood-relations in my pursuit of integration and healing weighs on me a great deal, actually.

I try not to internalize the rejection but...for some members of my family, I've become a mirror for everything about the amassed generational trauma that they don't want to face. And so, they are rejecting me rather than facing it.

[Long Pause].

While in a deep depression around how my blood-relations regard me, I read a quote by German psychotherapist, Bert Hellinger, that reframed the reaction of my family and affirmed that those who are trying to address the intergenerational trauma are indeed a precious part of that family (even if they are not well-liked). When you disrupt the status quo of silence and repression around trauma the family has endured and its subsequent manifestation of mental illness and abuse, you will be considered the black sheep, the troublemaker, the boat rocker but you are not.

Right Top: Spanish Mission Church, built 1717 after the Pueblo Revolt. Pecos Village, New Mexico, 2022.

Right Bottom: Spanish Mission Church in the background in contrast to the entrance to the Kiva featured on the right. Pecos Village, New Mexico, 2022.

Pecos Village, along Glorieta Pass,
New Mexico, 2022.

The so-called black sheep of the family are, in fact, hunters born of paths of liberation into the family tree. The members of a tree who do not conform to the norms or traditions of the family system, those who since childhood have constantly sought to revolutionize beliefs, going against the paths marked by family traditions, those criticized, judged, and even rejected, these are usually called to free the tree of repetitive stories that frustrate entire generations.

The black sheep, those who do not adapt, those who cry rebelliously, play a basic role within each family system, they repair, pick up and create new, and unfold branches in the family tree. Thanks to these members, our trees renew their roots. Its rebellion is fertile soil, its madness is water that nourishes, its stubbornness is new air, its passion is fire that re-ignites the light of the heart of the ancestors.

Uncountable repressed desires, unfulfilled dreams, the frustrated talents of our ancestors are manifested in the rebelliousness of these black sheep seeking fulfilment. The genealogical tree, by inertia will want to continue to maintain the castrating and toxic course of its trunk, which makes the task of our sheep a difficult and conflicting work. However, who would bring new flowers to our tree if it were not for them? Who would create new branches? Without them, the unfulfilled dreams of those who support the tree generations ago would die buried beneath their own roots. Let no one cause you to doubt, take care of your rarity as the most precious flower of your tree. You are the dream of all your ancestors.

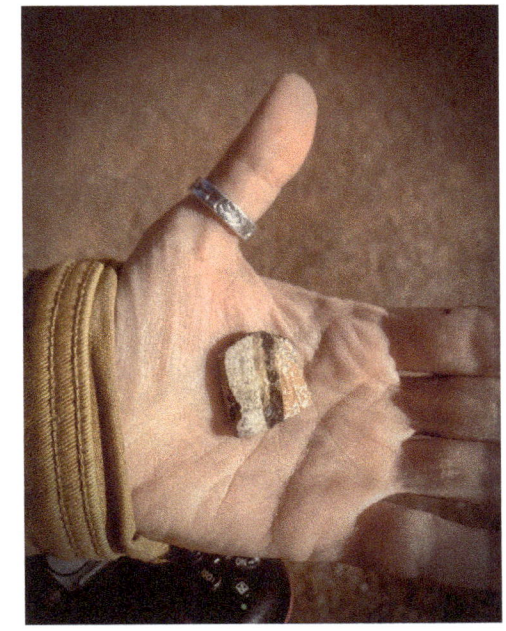

Left: Spanish Mission Church Ruins, Built 1717 after the Pueblo Revolt. Pecos Village, New Mexico, 2022.

Right: Self-portrait of the Photographer holding a fragment of Pueblo pottery found among the ruins. Pecos Village, New Mexico, 2022.

Frank: That is so spot-on! It sure seems to be the dynamic playing out on the national level as well with all of the backlash against critical race theory, the 1619 Project, and "anti-woke" sentiment. White supremacy and religious nationalism (which have no capacity to acknowledge realities outside itself) can only exist in a vacuum that suppresses such deeper questioning. It's the essence of denial.

Les: Oh, absolutely. Those issues you've mentioned *are* the intergenerational trauma dynamic being planned out on a global stage—the movements urging awareness, discussion, education, accountability, etc. around long-standing prejudice and trauma, and those who literally wish to maintain the status quo and outlaw discussion.

Denial is, by nature, truth-resistant. Whereas an objective perspective is affected by new information. Whereas denial is unaffected by new facts. I know that, when I am in denial, my mindset doesn't evolve with the introduction of new facts, because my mindset is not based in reality it is based on the story I am telling myself.

We live this truth on a global political scale—as the country stands divided by those of an objective perspective and those who are truth-resistant. Those of us whose perspective progresses with the introduction of new information and those of us who remain unmoved by facts because our mindset isn't based in reality, it is based in the stories we are telling ourselves and the stories we are being told by mass media, like these anti-woke movements. The intention behind facing intergenerational trauma is to try to identify what parts of our responses are being heavily influenced by our psychological conditioning so that we can work to distinguish the authentic response of our suppressed self and the response that is echoing the conditioning.

The merit of this approach is to move toward a life that is reflective of your most authentic self—the goal is to be free of mental conditioning and not merely be a complication of conditioning and coping mechanisms.

As a result of how Connor L. Wolfe came into the world, and my relentless drive to reckon with past trauma in the name of a more integrated and authentic future, I foresee my future works (under the name Connor Wolfe) being focused more on the visual arts; I've lived through words for twenty-four years. I see myself returning to photography and expanding into mini-doc formats. But, overall, continuing to voice my journey as a member of the generation who is trying to heal their own generational trauma. ...I will always be a storyteller, in all my processes.

"SHADOWS"

The Kiva, Pecos Village; New Mexico, 2022.

Frank: One of the things you and I share is a deep spirit-bond to the landscape of New Mexico. We've talked at length before about the multidimensional nature of the place. However, in recent years, you've had some very formative experiences there that have resulted in really shifting your "assemblage points", so to speak, to borrow a term from the old Carlos Castaneda books. Could you speak about this?

Les: If you read *To Lose the Madness* or know me personally, you have some idea of what it meant for me to return to Taos for this pivotal time in my journey.

All of my family is buried in New Mexico—I buried the twins in Cimmaron with the buffalo; I buried Mallory and I on Sandia; I buried my childhood in Abiquiu and—while I didn't know it at the time—I went to Taos to bury my immediate family who have chosen not to continue with me down my path.

Come to think of it, [Long Pause.]

I even buried myself there as well—Leslie M. Browning/L.M. Browning. I buried the name; I buried who I was conditioned to be; I buried the person everyone needed me to be; I buried the person long-held grudges were causing me to become; I buried the attachments I had around my future.

And, by that same hand, Connor was born in New Mexico, which I take deep comfort in...

Frank: This is the power of names and naming. We aren't just talking pen names here. This is the ending of one life and the beginning of another, and such rebirths are almost always preceded by breakdowns and breakthroughs of one kind or another.

Les: Right at the time I came out as nonbinary, I was suffering from a severe exacerbation of my CPTSD on the heels of a traumatizing/triggering run-in with the police department in my old hometown. The incident with the non-trauma-informed officers occurred in mid-June and that entire summer I was in what some shamanic cultures refer to as a dismemberment and re-assemblage; clinically speaking, I was suffering with my worst CPTSD exacerbation tantamount to a 12-week fugue state.

As the summer ended, I completed two intensive therapy programs and they had helped. I was more stable, but not anywhere near back on my feet. I knew I had to do the only thing that had ever helped me: Go West.

I posted a message on social media saying, I needed to pull up stakes and was looking for a place to post-up in the southwest. Within 48 hours, I had sublet a small studio from a fellow vagabond artist—in Taos of all places.

I dropped off the grid. I put my new lobo, Kiva, into the car and pointed it to New Mexico. I would say I stopped working but the truth was, I simply accepted I was not capable of working and hadn't been. So, I left work behind and went West with the singular focus of awe-seeking.

Hiking Frijoles Canyon, (Bandelier)
New Mexico, 2022.

Left: Inside a Pueblo Cliff Dwelling; Frijoles Canyon;
(Bandelier) New Mexico 2022.

Right: Self-portrait of the Photographer;
Frijoles Canyon; New Mexico, 2022.

Above: Decending the Cliff Dwelling,
Frijoles Canyon; New Mexico, 2022.

Frank: I love this term awe-seeking. What does "awe-seeking" look like for you?

Les: I think it looks vastly different for each individual, after all it is all based on what you find awe in. For me, it looks like an open road and having no obligations other than to myself—to anything other than where I want to go and what I want to do.

Frank: In my "world", I call it "sacred idleness", but in putting your own fine point on it, it sounds like it really involves movement for you—freedom?

Les: Yes. I completely understand though, I don't idle well. [Laughs.].

But freedom is just the vehicle; the awe is found in the landscape—the persistent beauty, the untouched wild spaces, the arcing spiral of time, the thin places, the primordial places...

Awe-seeking is driving until the road ends in front of a staggering red mesa, getting out of the car and walking into the wild unknown.

Frank: Speaking of arcs... That's all quite recent in the grand arc of time, and I know this must have catapulted you into the additional terrain of grief, not just the spirit-filled terrain of the land there.

Les: Oh my gosh, all of this is extraordinarily recent! [Laughs.] ...so much so that part of me was hesitant to put language around it and give this interview so early on. The rule is always not to talk about something you're still processing and I am breaking that rule. But I am allowing myself to have my feelings in this moment, even if I am still sifting through and integrating it all. However, I would say, even with the soft-understanding I have of the recent events in my life, I have become more and more aware of the overarching patterns in my behavior and my experiences.

"LONG ECHOES"
Frijoles Canyon, New Mexico 2022

Frank: In, *To Lose the Madness,* you spoke of "learning to carry the grief." What helps you carry the weight, which, as you say, is so present in your daily life?

Les: In that book, I chronicle coming to grips with the miscarriage of twins and the physical reality that I would never be a biological mother. I still agree with what I wrote—that the grief never goes away, we just learn how to carry it.

For reasons obvious to anyone who has spent a prolonged amount of time in *Nuevo México* (New Mexico), I am able to find enough space out there to hold all the feelings.

[Pause.] In all honestly, my grief runs deep—deeper than I can bear most days. Of all the tools in my toolbox, awe-seeking is the most powerful.

For me, awe is the counterbalance for trauma.

At the fever pitch, when things were the worst over the summer (when everyone was dying and I was coming to terms with my own repression), I couldn't hold all my feelings . . . let alone process them . . . let alone contain them.

I needed to go to New Mexico to find enough space to hold all the feelings I was having, and accept the orphanhood from my blood-relations that would be finalized while I was there.

My loyalty and dedication to my family's well-being are at the core of my being; so, to lose their companionship in my journey was devastating. New Mexico—the landscape, the ancestral energy—it provides enough awe that it can hold the heaviest of grief.

Different landscapes are like different religions—they are each paths that lead to the same primordial truth—some just speak more to us than others. New England has been my religion for the bulk of my life, but my path into myself, into healing, into evolving cuts through the high desert of the Southwest.

Top: "**UNTIL THE WHEELS FALL OFF**"
Red River; New Mexico, 2022.

Bottom: Vallas Caldera;
Jemez Mountains; New Mexico, 2022.

ENDNOTES

1   Sho, Terushi. "Kintsugi: Japan's Ancient Art of Embracing Imperfection." Accessed April 1, 2023. https://www.bbc.com/travel/article/20210107-kintsugi-japans-ancient-art-of-embracing-imperfection.

2   Kumu Hina. https://kumuhina.com/.

3   It would be a gross misrepresentation not to recognize the prejudice against those of nonbinary gender within the global landscape. For example, if you're *Bakla*, your rights/role in the culture are limited. In India, the *Hijras* are relegated to outcasts and are reduced to survive through begging.

4   Fewster, P. H. (n.d.). Two-spirit community. Researching for LGBTQ Health. Retrieved February 24, 2023, from https://lgbtqhealth.ca/community/two-spirit.php

5   "Two Spirit and LGBTQ Idenitites: Today and Centuries Ago - HRC." Human Rights Campaign. Accessed March 24, 2023. https://www.hrc.org/news/two-spirit-and-lgbtq-idenitites-today-and-centuries-ago.

6   "When did girls start wearing pink?" by Jeanne Maglaty, *Smithsonian Magazine,* Apr. 7, 2011

7   YouTube. (2021, November 30). Brené Brown on shame, perfectionism and vulnerability | *happy place podcast*. YouTube. Retrieved March 7, 2023, from https://m.youtube.com/watch?v=iFuavxXFNy8

8   Rothberg, Emma. "Sylvia Rivera." National Women's History Museum. Accessed March 20, 2023. https://www.womenshistory.org/education-resources/biographies/sylvia-rivera.

9   Chait, Jonathan. "CPAC Speaker Michael Knowles Urges Eradication of Trans Rights." *Intelligencer,* March 6, 2023. https://nymag.com/intelligencer/2023/03/michael-knowles-at-cpac-urges-eradication-of-trans-rights.html.

10   Best resource on CPTSD: Walker, Pete. *Complex PTSD: From Surviving to Thriving: A Guide and Map for Recovering from Childhood Trauma.* Lafayette, CA: Azure Coyote, 2013.

11   Though, it should be mentioned that my choice to keep part of my name is unique in the trans community. Usually, if a member of the transgender community chooses to change their name, the old name you leave behind is considered your "dead name." Using someone's dead name is deeply insulting.

12   A good resource to start with if you're interested in learning more about psychedelic therapy is: Pollan, M. (2018). *How to change your mind the new science of psychedelics.* Allen Lane. *Also adapted into a NETFLIX documentary.*

13   "Gerald's Tree I, 1937 by Georgia O'Keeffe - Paper Print - Georgia O'keeffe Museum Custom Prints - Custom Prints and Framing from the Georgia O'Keeffe Museum." Georgia O'Keeffe Museum Custom Prints. Accessed April 2, 2023. https://prints.okeeffemuseum.org/detail/463090/okeeffe-geralds-tree-i-1937.

"REACH"

Abiquiú, New Mexico, 2022.

ACKNOWLEDGEMENTS

This book is dedicated to several people . . .

To the 19 Pueblo tribes of *Nuevo México*. Each pueblo is a sovereign nation. The landscape I wandered gathering awe and strength is rightfully yours and has been taken through violent colonization. I am in awe of your endurance. I am grateful for your blessing to come be in-space with your landscape and the energy your ancestors hold there still. Ten percent of the proceeds from this work will be donated to The Indian Pueblo Cultural Center in Albuquerque. The IPCC serves as a gathering place where Pueblo Culture is celebrated through creative and cultural experiences, while providing economic opportunities to Pueblo and local communities.

To my closest partners—both present and past—Sara, Kelly, and Andy. You all showed up for me when everyone else walked away. Thank you for doing your respective work so we could meet in the middle and move forward. You each stood by me when I was undiagnosed, under-medicated, over-medicated, suicidal, unemployable, unhoused, and unhinged. I am grateful for each of you.

To my *lost boys* of childhood: Nick, Scott, Kenny, Brandy, Megan, Little Nick, Christina, Ryan, Steven, Brian, Phil, Donny, Seth, Rose, Sage...and so, so many more. You are my family.

To my brother, Frank Inzan Owen, for assisting in this work of alchemy and awe. Your kinship has been invaluable to me over the years.

To my brother, Jason, for bringing publishing into my life and giving me the tools to bring my work and the works of so many others into a market that otherwise wouldn't have made room for us. Since the day we had our first meeting—at that fairtrade coffeehouse in the North End—I have been grateful to know you. You set a high standard, and we are all the better for it.

To Marie & Larue. Your entrance into my life is a story I will happily tell over and over again. You've gathered many of us castoff children. You helped me reach beyond poverty toward my dreams and you taught me what community is.

To fellow roamers Sharon Vine and Mike Ferrara for inviting me to Taos for the first time. And to Thaddeus Jacobs for inviting me to Taos the second time and giving me a home base for these months of rambling.

To B. for seeing Connor before I fully could and making space to explore.

To the Georgia O'Keeffe Museum in Santa Fe and the O'Keeffe Home & Studio in Abiquiú for their unwavering dedication to Georgia's life and legacy and the generosity in which they share their knowledge.

To the authors & editors I work with who inspire me daily: Heidi Barr, Iris Graville, David K. Leff, Kristen Williams, Gary Whited, Gunilla Norris, Stephen Drew, Theodore Richards, James Scott Smith, Walker Abel, Burt Bradley, Gail Collins-Ranadive, Aimée Medina Carr, Will Falk, Gwendolyn Morgan, Stephen Trimble, Brooke & Terry Williams, Robin Cutler, Karla Olson, Angela Bole, Brooke Warner, Karen Pavlicin, Elissa Sweet, and Robert Broder.

To the teachers who have been true mentors: to the librarians at the Westerly Public Library for providing me with my first education; to the librarians at Widener Library for allowing me to read the notes in the margins; and to the professors at Harvard who most-deeply inspired me including Samantha Appleton, Nick Manley, and Christina Thompson.

Finally, to all my communities—the lesbian community, the queer community, the nonbinary community, the transgender community, the sober community, the CPTSD Community, the Survivors of Suicide Attempt community, the poet & spoken word community, the road-lifers community, high-desert roamers, the homesteading & farming community, and to the communities yet-to-be formed. We need a village.

CONTRIBUTORS

FRANK INZAN OWEN (he/him) is a Wayfarer of a Nature-oriented spiritual path shaped by the seasons, mountains-and-forests meditation, methods of "inner archaeology" and dreaming-while-awake, and "practice-hints" found in the lives and verses of various Wayfaring poets of the Far East. The author of three books of poetry published by Homebound Publications, *The School of Soft-Attention, The Temple of Warm Harmony,* and *Stirrup of the Sun & Moon,* when not tending an organic vegetable garden or hillwalking, he facilitates a form of Jungian-informed inner work he calls contemplative soulwork through his organization, The School of Soft-Attention (schoolofsoftattention.com), and curates The Poet's Dreamingbody podcast and Substack (thepoetsdreamingbody.com).

CONNOR L. WOLFE (they/them), TEDx Speaker and founder of *Wayfarer Magazine,* author of *Drive Through the Night* and numerous other works under the pen name, L.M. Browning. Connor's hybrid of introspective travel writing and visual art focuses on the alchemizing of trauma through active awe-seeking and a re-wilding of one's life and self.

Wolfe serves on the State of Connecticut's/NAMI's Lived Experience Committee and received national certification as a Peer Facilitator for Survivor of Suicide Attempt Groups through the Didi Hirsch Mental Health Services Foundation in Los Angeles. Connor is a vocal advocate for the CPTSD community and new Psilocybin therapies for treatment of severe cases. They are a graduate of Harvard University and a longtime student of *vipassana* meditation and *koryu bujutsu.*

Living primarily on the road, in their overlanding-rigged obsidian-black Subaru Forester, (affectionally called, Pearl) Connor and their coydog, Kiva, divide their time between Northern New Mexico and Wayfarer Farm in the Berkshire Mountains of Massachusetts.

"RISTRAS"
Santa Fe, New Mexico 2022

WAYFARER MAGAZINE

SPECIAL EDITION